No A.R,

ROMAN REIGNS:
THE BIG DOG

TEDDY BORTH

abdopublishing.com

Published by Abdo Zoom, a division of ABDO, P.O. Box 398166, Minneapolis, Minnesota 55439. Copyright © 2018 by Abdo Consulting Group, Inc. International copyrights reserved in all countries. No part of this book may be reproduced in any form without written permission from the publisher.

Printed in the United States of America, North Mankato, Minnesota.
092017
012018

Photo Credits: AllWrestlingSuperstars.com, AP Images, Getty Images, Icon Sportswire, iStock, Shutterstock, ©Megan Elice Meadows CC BY-SA 2.0 p. 14
Production Contributors: Kenny Abdo, Jennie Forsberg, Grace Hansen
Design Contributors: Dorothy Toth, Neil Klinepier

Publisher's Cataloging-in-Publication Data

Names: Borth, Teddy, author.
Title: Roman Reigns: the big dog / by Teddy Borth.
Other titles: The big dog
Description: Minneapolis, Minnesota: Abdo Zoom, 2018. | Series: Wrestling biographies | Includes online resource and index.
Identifiers: LCCN 2017939294 | ISBN 9781532121111 (lib.bdg.)
    ISBN 9781532122231 (ebook) | ISBN 9781532122798 (Read-to-Me ebook)
Subjects: LCSH: Reigns, Roman (Leati Anoa'i), d1985- --Juvenile literature.
    Wrestlers--Juvenile literature. | Biography--Juvenile literature.
Classification: DDC 796.812 [B]--dc23
LC record available at https://lccn.loc.gov/2017939294

TABLE OF CONTENTS

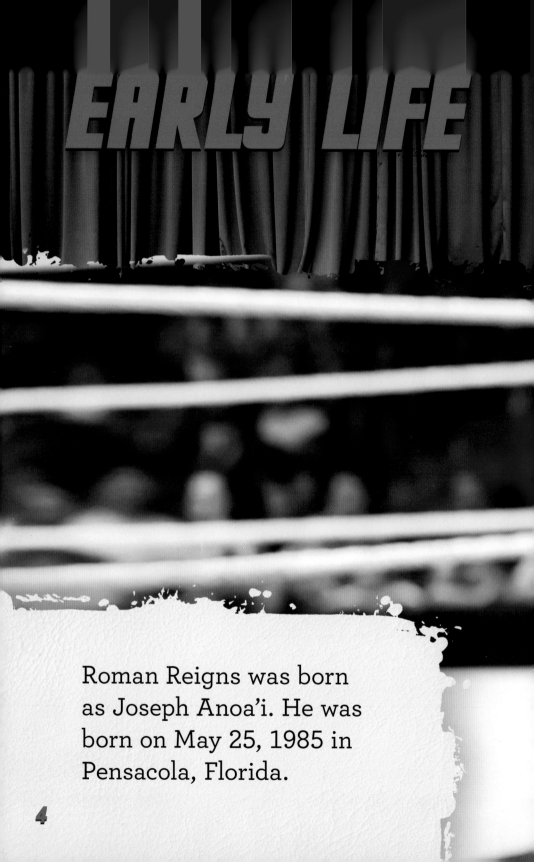

EARLY LIFE

Roman Reigns was born as Joseph Anoa'i. He was born on May 25, 1985 in Pensacola, Florida.

4

Reigns wanted to play
football. He joined
a Canadian Football
League team. He
played five games for
the Edmonton Eskimos.

FLORIDA CHAMPIONSHIP WRESTLING

Reigns joined Florida Championship Wrestling (FCW) in July 2010. WWE used FCW to train wrestlers. He first wrestled under the name Roman Leakee.

FCW was changed to **NXT** in 2012. Roman Leakee changed his name to Roman Reigns. He **debuted** on October 31, 2012.

THE SHIELD

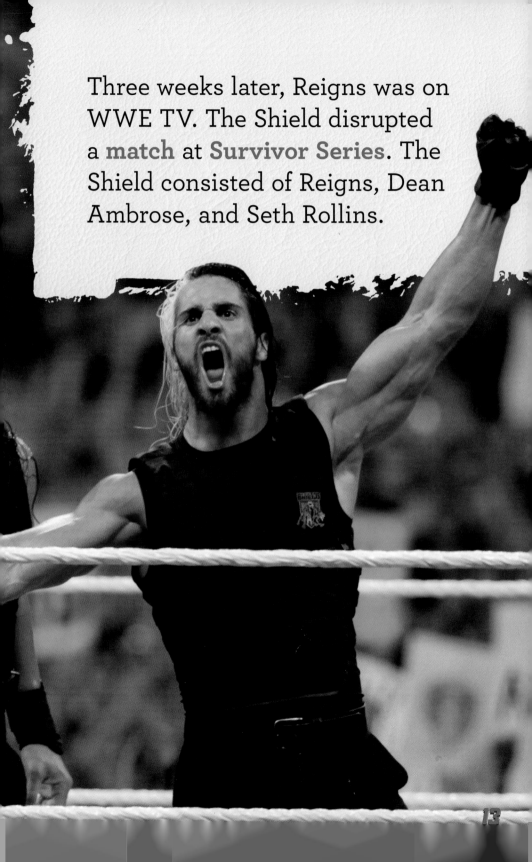

Three weeks later, Reigns was on WWE TV. The Shield disrupted a **match** at **Survivor Series**. The Shield consisted of Reigns, Dean Ambrose, and Seth Rollins.

13

Reigns won his first **title** in WWE as a **tag team**. He won it with Rollins on May 19, 2013.

WWE CHAMPIONSHIP

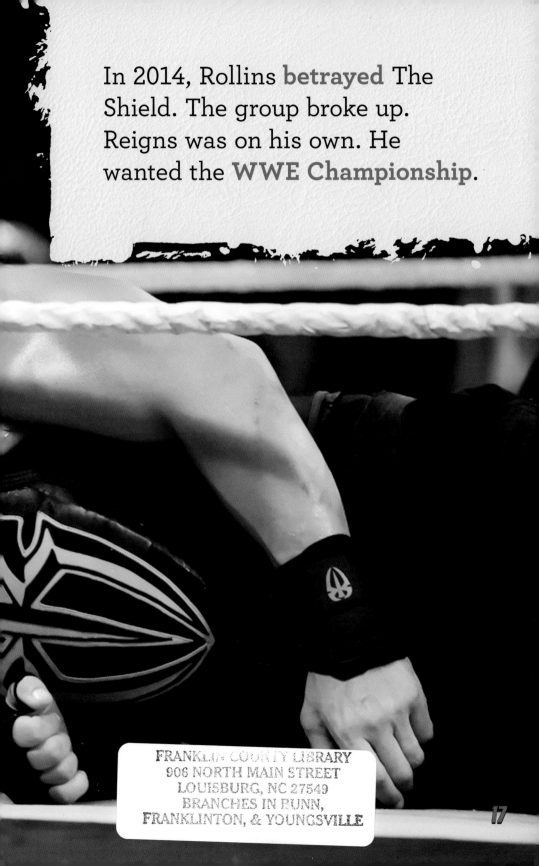

In 2014, Rollins **betrayed** The Shield. The group broke up. Reigns was on his own. He wanted the **WWE Championship**.

In November 2015, Reigns won a tournament to become WWE champion for the first time!

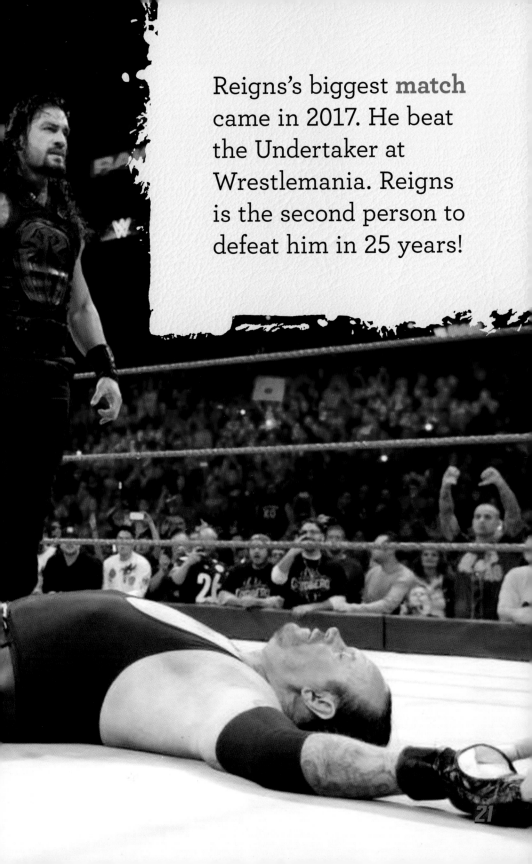

Reigns's biggest **match** came in 2017. He beat the Undertaker at Wrestlemania. Reigns is the second person to defeat him in 25 years!

21

GLOSSARY

betray – to turn against, lie to, or hurt.

debut – to appear for the first time.

match – a competition in which wrestlers fight against each other.

NXT – WWE's developmental brand. WWE uses NXT to help wrestlers learn and grow before bringing them to the main roster.

Survivor Series – a major WWE show held every year in November.

tag team – a division made up of teams of two people. Wrestlers tag their partner to get in and out of the match.

title – the position of being the best in that division.

WWE Championship – the top prize in WWE.

ONLINE RESOURCES

Booklinks
NONFICTION NETWORK
FREE! ONLINE NONFICTION RESOURCES

To learn more about Roman Reigns, please visit abdobooklinks.com. These links are routinely monitored and updated to provide the most current information available.

INDEX